THE LEFT-HANDED CASEBOOK

by **Dave Rubin** and **Matt Scharfglass**

Table of Contents

Project Manager: Dave Rubin
Project Coordinator: Karl Bork
Book Art Design: Carmen Fortunato
Technical Editor: Albert Nigro
Engraver: Adrian Alvarez

WARNER BROS. PUBLICATIONS
Warner Music Group
An AOL Time Warner Company
USA: 15800 NW 48th Avenue, Miami, FL 33014

WARNER/CHAPPELL MUSIC
CANADA: 15800 N.W. 48th AVENUE
MIAMI, FLORIDA 33014
SCANDINAVIA: P.O. BOX 533, VENDEVAGEN 85 B
S-182 15, DANDERYD, SWEDEN
AUSTRALIA: P.O. BOX 353
3 TALAVERA ROAD, NORTH RYDE N.S.W. 2113
ASIA: THE PENINSULA OFFICE TOWER, 12th FLOOR
18 MIDDLE ROAD
TSIM SHA TSUI, KOWLOON, HONG KONG

ITALY: VIA CAMPANIA, 12
20098 S. GIULIANO MILANESE (MI)
ZONA INDUSTRIALE SESTO ULTERIANO
SPAIN: MAGALLANES, 25
28015 MADRID
FRANCE: CARISCH MUSICOM
25, RUE D'HAUTEVILLE, 75010 PARIS

INTERNATIONAL MUSIC PUBLICATIONS LIMITED
ENGLAND: GRIFFIN HOUSE,
161 HAMMERSMITH ROAD, LONDON W6 8BS
GERMANY: MARSTALLSTR. 8, D-80539 MÜNCHEN
DENMARK: DANMUSIK, VOGNMAGERGADE 7
DK 1120 KÖBENHAVNK

Introduction

Jimi Hendrix once said, "Learn your chords and everything else will follow." Though he was not the first to offer that sage advice, he certainly practiced what he preached. Jimi was a master rhythm guitarist who learned the correct chords through years of playing experience.

The correct chords. That is part of the secret to becoming a great guitarist. There are literally *thousands* of chords that can be played up and down the fingerboard, but what you need to know are the best and most useful. This book is your guide to that inside knowledge.

The 11 most essential chord types are pictured in grids starting in C and continuing through all 12 keys. Open chords, barre chords and hip four-note voicings are presented, giving you a choice of fingerings and location on the neck, for a total of 48 voicings in each key.

Whether you play rock, blues, jazz, country or any other style of guitar music, the correct chord information is contained within. By keeping this handy chord guide in your gig bag or guitar case, you will always have the chord form you need, when you need it, to sound great in any situation.

How to Use This Book

- Chords found within the first five frets do not have a fret number.
- X's indicate strings to be muted or not strummed.
- O's indicate open strings to be strummed.
- A box around a note identifies it as the root.

- The numbers under the grids indicate fingerings 1=index, 2=middle, 3=ring, 4 =pinky.
- An arched line indicates a barre, usually with the index finger.

- A barre below other indicated fingers is usually played with the ring finger.

Basic Chord Theory

Chords are derived from *chord formulas*. If that gives you a vision of a scientist working in a dark laboratory on something mysterious and beyond your grasp, you can relax. Chord formulas are founded on the simplest of math principles. If you can count to eight, and by extension 13, you can understand basic chord theory.

Chords are constructed from the major scale, also called the diatonic scale or Ionian mode. This is the "do-re-mi" scale we all know. Every key (there are 12) has its own major scale consisting of eight notes. Each note is given a number. These numbers are referred to as scale degrees. Shown below is the C-major scale with the scale degrees underneath. The first note (1) is usually called the root, with the succeeding notes known as the 2nd, 3rd, 4th, 5th, 6th, 7th and octave (the same note as the root, one octave higher).

C	D	E	F	G	A	B	C
1	2	3	4	5	6	7	8

By combining various combinations of notes from the major scale, we create chords. Listed below are the formulas for the 11 chords diagrammed in each key. Keep in mind the following points as you go through the list:

- ♭ = lower that note by one fret.
  ♯ = raise that note by one fret.
  Ex: ♭3rd. In the key of C you would lower E to E♭.
- The notes repeat, in the same order, past the octave up to 13. Ex: C9. If you count past the octave (C), the next note, D, is the 9th note.
- Many chords double and even triple some of the notes from the formula for a fuller sound. Ex: A major barre chord may have three root notes. Likewise, some chords with more than four notes (13th) are often played without certain notes (5th, 7th, 9th) to make the fingering easier.

major = 1, 3, 5
minor = 1, ♭3, 5
dominant 7 = 1, 3, 5, ♭7
major 7 = 1, 3, 5, 7
minor 7 = 1, ♭3, 5, ♭7
9th = 1, 3, 5, 7, 9
13th = 1, 3, 5, 7, 9, 13
6th = 1, 3, 5, 6
sus 4 (suspended 4th) = 1, 4, 5
augmented = 1, 3, ♯5
diminished 7 = 1, ♭3, ♭5, ♭♭7 (6)

The 12 Major Scales

C	D	E	F	G	A	B	C
Db	Eb	F	Gb	Ab	Bb	C	Db
D	E	F#	G	A	B	C#	D
Eb	F	G	Ab	Bb	C	D	Eb
E	F#	G#	A	B	C#	D#	E
F	G	A	Bb	C	D	E	F
Gb	Ab	Bb	Cb	Db	Eb	F	Gb
G	A	B	C	D	E	F#	G
Ab	Bb	C	Db	Eb	F	G	Ab
A	B	C#	D	E	F#	G#	A
Bb	C	D	Eb	F	G	A	Bb
B	C#	D#	E	F#	G#	A#	B

The Notes on the Fingerboard

Fret	Ⓔ	Ⓑ	Ⓖ	Ⓓ	Ⓐ	Ⓔ
1	F	C	G#	D#	A#	F
2	F#	C#	A	E	B	F#
3	G	D	A#	F	C	G
4	G#	D#	B	F#	C#	G#
5	A	E	C	G	D	A
6	A#	F	C#	G#	D#	A#
7	B	F#	D	A	E	B
8	C	G	D#	A#	F	C
9	C#	G#	E	B	F#	C#
10	D	A	F	C	G	D
11	D#	A#	F#	C#	G#	D#
12	E	B	G	D	A	E
13	F	C	G#	D#	A#	F
14	F#	C#	A	E	B	F#
15	G	D	A#	F	C	G
16	G#	D#	B	F#	C#	G#
17	A	E	C	G	D	A
18	A#	F	C#	G#	D#	A#

Hints for Choosing the Correct Chords

One of the joys of playing the guitar is the nearly infinite number of ways to combine chords. But, like choosing your words, if you do it carefully you will be able to express yourself with confidence. As with good grammar, there are certain guidelines that will help you in crafting flowing, harmonious musical statements.

Open Chords

A simple but sure-fire concept is the use of open chords with their ringing open strings to maintain *continuity* in a progression. This can be particularly effective when the lowest open string is the root of each chord.

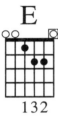

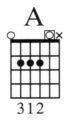

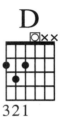

Common Tones

Combining chords that share some of the same notes (common tones) makes for fluid transitions.

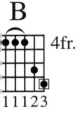

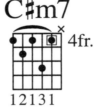

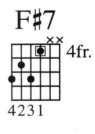

Bass Notes

Keeping the bass note of each chord on the same string and close together can make it sound as if a bass is accompanying you.

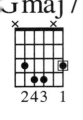

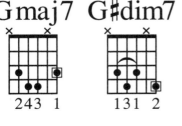

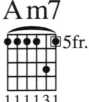

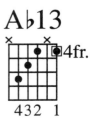

Key of C

C major
(C)

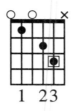

1 23

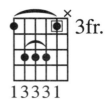

3fr.

13331

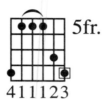

5fr.

411123

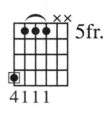

5fr.

4111

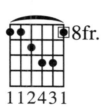

8fr.

112431

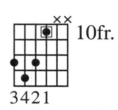

10fr.

3421

C minor
(Cm, Cmi, Cmin, C-)

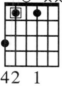

42 1

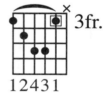

3fr.

12431

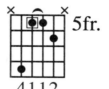

5fr.

4112

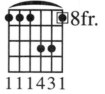

8fr.

111431

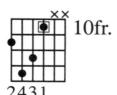

10fr.

2431

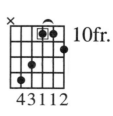

10fr.

43112

8

C dominant 7
(C7)

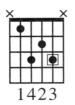

1423

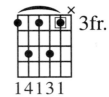

14131 3fr.

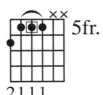

2111 5fr.

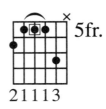

21113 5fr.

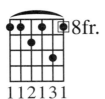

112131 8fr.

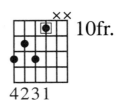

4231 10fr.

C major 7
(Cmaj7, CMaj7, CΔ7, *C7)

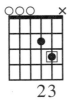

23

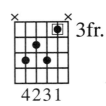

4231 3fr.

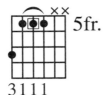

3111 5fr.

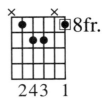

243 1 8fr.

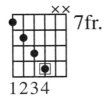

1234 7fr.

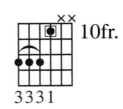

3331 10fr.

* Not recommended

9

C minor 7
(Cm7, Cmi7, Cmin7, C -7)

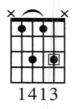

1413

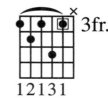

3fr.

12131

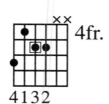

4fr.

4132

8fr.

111131

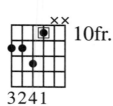

10fr.

3241

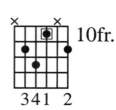

10fr.

341 2

C dominant 9
(C9)

33312

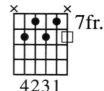

7fr.

4231

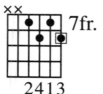

7fr.

2413

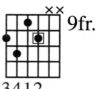

9fr.

3412

C dominant 13
(C13)

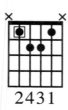

2431

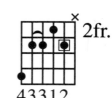

2fr.

43312

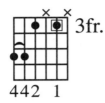 3fr.

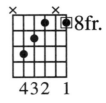 8fr.

C major 6
(C6)

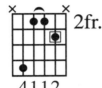 2fr.

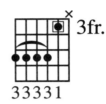 3fr.

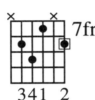 7fr.

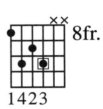 8fr.

C suspended 4
(Csus, Csus4)

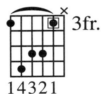 3fr.

 8fr.

C augmented
(Caug, C+)

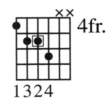 4fr.

C diminished 7
(Cdim7, C°7)

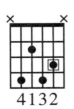

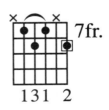 7fr.

Key of D♭

D♭ major
(D♭)

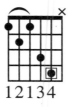

12134

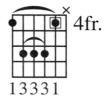

4fr.

13331

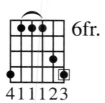

6fr.

411123

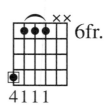

6fr.

4111

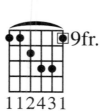

9fr.

112431

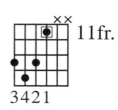

11fr.

3421

D♭ minor
(D♭m, D♭mi, D♭min, D♭-)

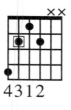

4312

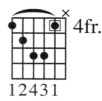

4fr.

12431

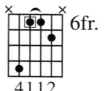

6fr.

4112

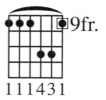

9fr.

111431

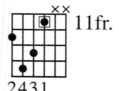

11fr.

2431

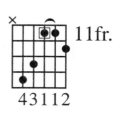

11fr.

43112

D♭ dominant 7
(D♭7)

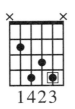
1423

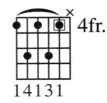
4fr.
14131

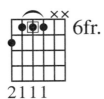
6fr.
2111

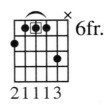
6fr.
21113

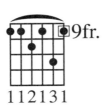
9fr.
112131

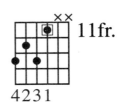
11fr.
4231

D♭ major 7
(D♭maj7, D♭Maj7, D♭Δ7, *D♭7)

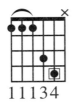
11134

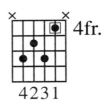
4fr.
4231

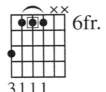
6fr.
3111

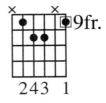
9fr.
243 1

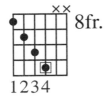
8fr.
1234

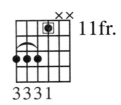
11fr.
3331

* Not recommended

D♭ minor 7
(D♭m7, D♭mi7, D♭min7, D♭-7)

1413

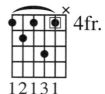

4fr.

12131

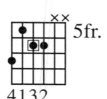

5fr.

4132

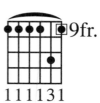

9fr.

111131

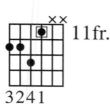

11fr.

3241

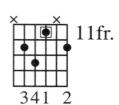

11fr.

341 2

D♭ dominant 9
(D♭9)

33312

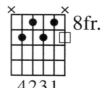

8fr.

4231

8fr.

2413

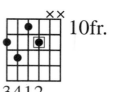

10fr.

3412

D♭ dominant 13
(D♭13)

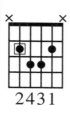

2431

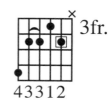

3fr.

43312

(D♭13)

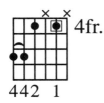 4fr.
442 1

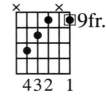 9fr.
432 1

D♭ major 6
(D♭6)

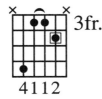 3fr.
4112

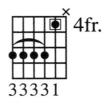 4fr.
33331

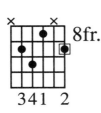 8fr.
341 2

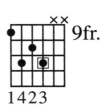 9fr.
1423

D♭ suspended 4
(D♭sus, D♭sus4)

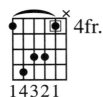 4fr.
14321

 9fr.
114311

D♭ augmented
(D♭aug, D♭+)

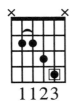
1123

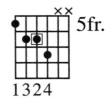 5fr.
1324

D♭ diminished 7
(D♭dim7, D♭°7)

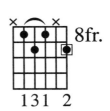 3fr.
4132

8fr.
131 2

15

Key of D

D major
(D)

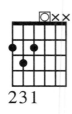

231

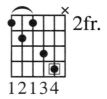

2fr.

12134

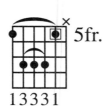

5fr.

13331

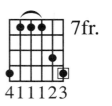

7fr.

411123

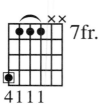

7fr.

4111

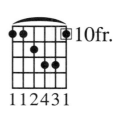

10fr.

112431

D minor
(Dm, Dmi, Dmin, D-)

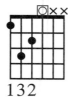

132

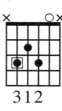

312

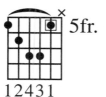

5fr.

12431

7fr.

4112

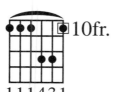

10fr.

111431

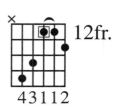

12fr.

43112

D dominant 7
(D7)

3 1 2

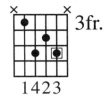

3fr.

1 4 2 3

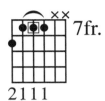

7fr.

2 1 1 1

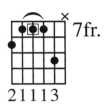

7fr.

2 1 1 1 3

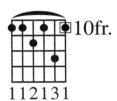

10fr.

1 1 2 1 3 1

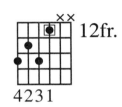

12fr.

4 2 3 1

D major 7
(Dmaj7, DMaj7, DΔ7, *D⁷)

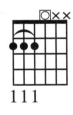

1 1 1

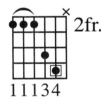

2fr.

1 1 1 3 4

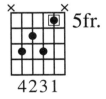

5fr.

4 2 3 1

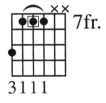

7fr.

3 1 1 1

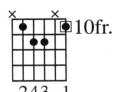

10fr.

2 4 3 1

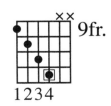

9fr.

1 2 3 4

* Not recommended

17

D minor 7
(Dm7, Dmi7, Dmin7, D-7)

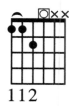

112

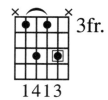

3fr.

1413

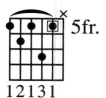

5fr.

12131

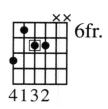

6fr.

4132

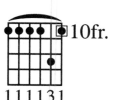

10fr.

111131

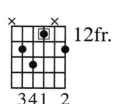

12fr.

341 2

D dominant 9
(D9)

4fr.

33312

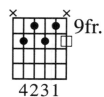

9fr.

4231

9fr.

2413

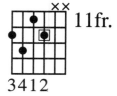

11fr.

3412

D dominant 13
(D13)

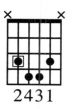

2431

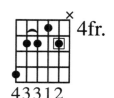

4fr.

43312

18

(D13)

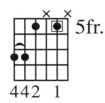 5fr.
4 4 2   1

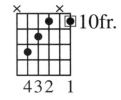 10fr.
4 3 2   1

D major 6
(D6)

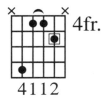 4fr.
4 1 1 2

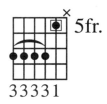 5fr.
3 3 3 3 1

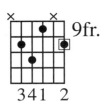 9fr.
3 4 1   2

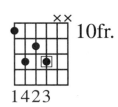 10fr.
1 4 2 3

D suspended 4
(Dsus, Dsus4)

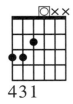
4 3 1

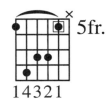 5fr.
1 4 3 2 1

D augmented
(Daug, D+)

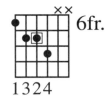 3fr.
1 1 2 3

 6fr.
1 3 2 4

D diminished 7
(Ddim7, D°7)

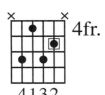 4fr.
4 1 3 2

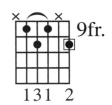 9fr.
1 3 1   2

19

Key of E♭

E♭ major
(E♭)

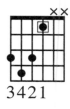
3 4 2 1

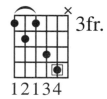
3fr.
1 2 1 3 4

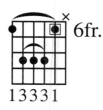
6fr.
1 3 3 3 1

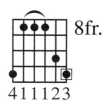
8fr.
4 1 1 1 2 3

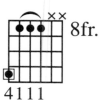
8fr.
4 1 1 1

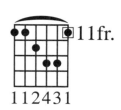
11fr.
1 1 2 4 3 1

E♭ minor
(E♭m, E♭mi, E♭min, E♭-)

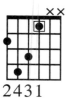
2 4 3 1

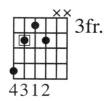
3fr.
4 3 1 2

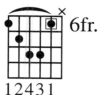
6fr.
1 2 4 3 1

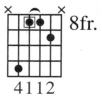
8fr.
4 1 1 2

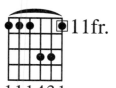
11fr.
1 1 1 4 3 1

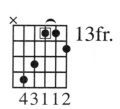
13fr.
4 3 1 1 2

E♭ dominant 7
(E♭7)

4231

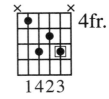
4fr.
1423

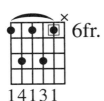
6fr.
14131

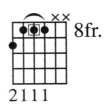
8fr.
2111

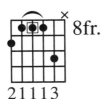
8fr.
21113

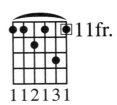
11fr.
112131

E♭ major 7
(E♭maj7, E♭Maj7, E♭Δ7, *E♭7)

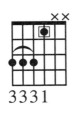
3331

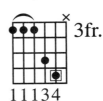
3fr.
11134

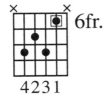
6fr.
4231

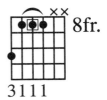
8fr.
3111

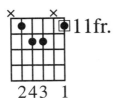
11fr.
243 1

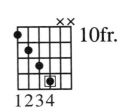
10fr.
1234

* Not recommended

E♭ minor 7
(E♭m7, E♭mi7, E♭min7, E♭-7)

3241

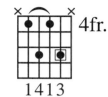

4fr.

1413

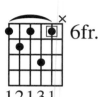

6fr.

12131

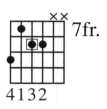

7fr.

4132

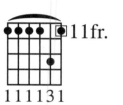

11fr.

111131

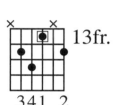

13fr.

341 2

E♭ dominant 9
(E♭9)

5fr.

33312

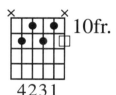

10fr.

4231

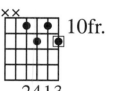

10fr.

2413

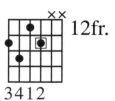

12fr.

3412

E♭ dominant 13
(E♭13)

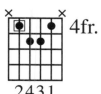

4fr.

2431

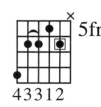

5fr.

43312

(E♭13)

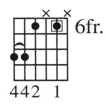 6fr.

4 4 2   1

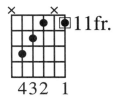 11fr.

4 3 2   1

E♭ major 6
(E♭6)

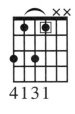

4 1 3 1

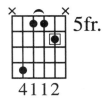 5fr.

4 1 1 2

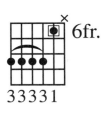 6fr.

3 3 3 3 1

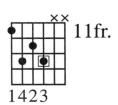 11fr.

1 4 2 3

E♭ suspended 4
(E♭sus, E♭sus4)

 6fr.

1 4 3 2 1

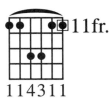 11fr.

1 1 4 3 1 1

E♭ augmented
(E♭aug, E♭+)

 4fr.

1 1 2 3

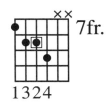 7fr.

1 3 2 4

E♭ diminished 7
(E♭dim7, E♭°7)

4 2 3 1

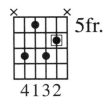 5fr.

4 1 3 2

23

Key of E

E major
(E)

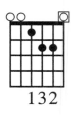

132

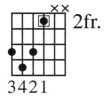

2fr.

3421

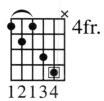

4fr.

12134

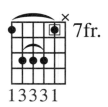

7fr.

13331

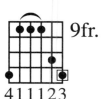

9fr.

411123

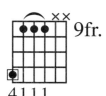

9fr.

4111

E minor
(Em, Emi, Emin, E-)

21

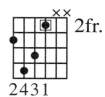

2fr.

2431

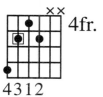

4fr.

4312

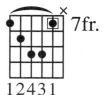

7fr.

12431

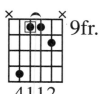

9fr.

4112

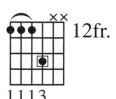

12fr.

1113

24

E dominant 7
(E7)

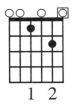

1 2

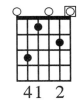

41 2

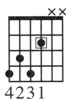

4231

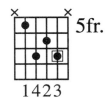

5fr.

1423

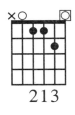

7fr.

14131

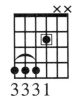

9fr.

2111

E major 7
(Emaj7, EMaj7, EΔ7, *E7)

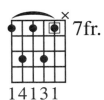

213

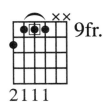

3331

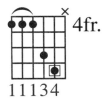

4fr.

11134

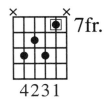

7fr.

4231

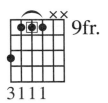

9fr.

3111

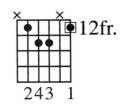

12fr.

243 1

* Not recommended

E minor 7
(Em7, Emi7, Emin7, E-7)

1

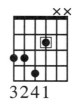

3241

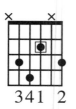

341 2

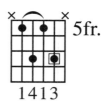

5fr.

1413

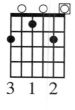

7fr.

12131

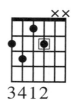

8fr.

4132

E dominant 9
(E9)

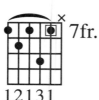

3 1 2

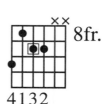

3412

6fr.

33312

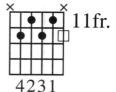

11fr.

4231

E dominant 13
(E13)

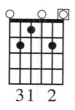

31 2

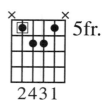

5fr.

2431

(E13)

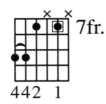 7fr.

442 1

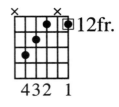 12fr.

432 1

E major 6
(E6)

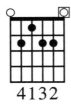

4132

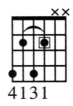

4131

 6fr.

4112

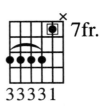 7fr.

33331

E suspended 4
(Esus, Esus4)

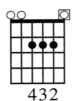

432

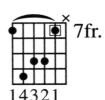 7fr.

14321

E augmented
(Eaug, E+)

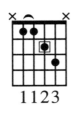

1123

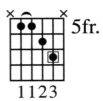 5fr.

1123

E diminished 7
(Edim7, E°7)

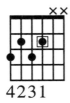

4231

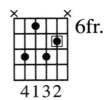 6fr.

4132

Key of F

F major
(F)

1 1 2 4 3 1

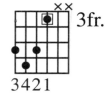

3fr.

3 4 2 1

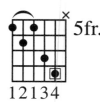

5fr.

1 2 1 3 4

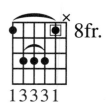

8fr.

1 3 3 3 1

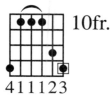

10fr.

4 1 1 1 2 3

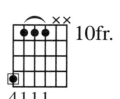

10fr.

4 1 1 1

F minor
(Fm, Fmi, Fmin, F-)

1 1 1 4 3 1

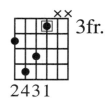

3fr.

2 4 3 1

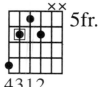

5fr.

4 3 1 2

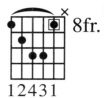

8fr.

1 2 4 3 1

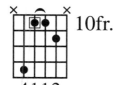

10fr.

4 1 1 2

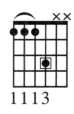

1 1 1 3

F dominant 7
(F7)

1 1 2 1 3 1

1 4 2 1 3 1

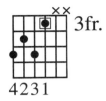

3fr.

4 2 3 1

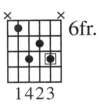

6fr.

1 4 2 3

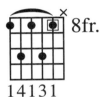

8fr.

1 4 1 3 1

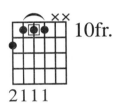

10fr.

2 1 1 1

F major 7
(Fmaj7, FMaj7, F△7, *F7)

2 4 3 1

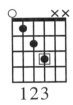

1 2 3

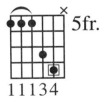

3fr.

3 3 3 1

5fr.

1 1 1 3 4

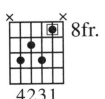

8fr.

4 2 3 1

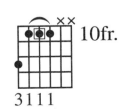

10fr.

3 1 1 1

* Not recommended

29

F minor 7
(Fm7, Fmi7, Fmin7, F-7)

1 1 1 1 3 1

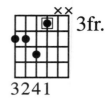

3fr.

3 2 4 1

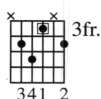

3fr.

3 4 1 2

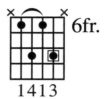

6fr.

1 4 1 3

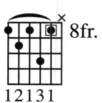

8fr.

1 2 1 3 1

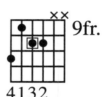

9fr.

4 1 3 2

F dominant 9
(F9)

4 1 2 1 3 1

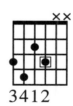

3 4 1 2

7fr.

3 3 3 1 2

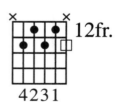

12fr.

4 2 3 1

F dominant 13
(F13)

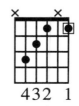

1 4 2 1 3 1

4 3 2 1

(F13)

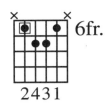

6fr.

2431

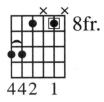

8fr.

442 1

F major 6
(F6)

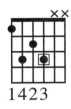

1423

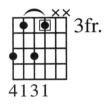

3fr.

4131

7fr.

4112

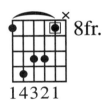

8fr.

33331

F suspended 4
(Fsus, Fsus4)

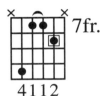

114321

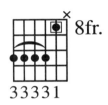

8fr.

14321

F augmented
(Faug, F+)

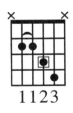

1123

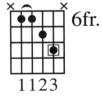

6fr.

1123

F diminished 7
(Fdim7, F°7)

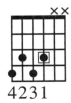

4231

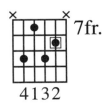

7fr.

4132

Key of G♭

G♭ major
(G♭)

1 1 2 4 3 1

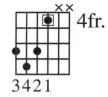

4fr.

3 4 2 1

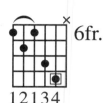

6fr.

1 2 1 3 4

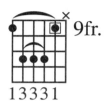

9fr.

1 3 3 3 1

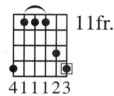

11fr.

4 1 1 1 2 3

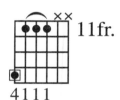

11fr.

4 1 1 1

G♭ minor
(G♭m, G♭mi, G♭min, G♭-)

1 1 1 4 3 1

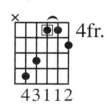

4fr.

4 3 1 1 2

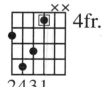

4fr.

2 4 3 1

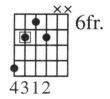

6fr.

4 3 1 2

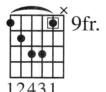

9fr.

1 2 4 3 1

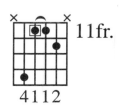

11fr.

4 1 1 2

32

Gb dominant 7
(Gb7)

112131

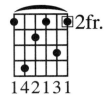

2fr.

142131

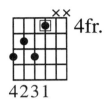

4fr.

4231

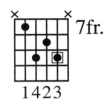

7fr.

1423

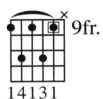

9fr.

14131

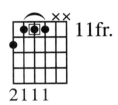

11fr.

2111

Gb major 7
(Gbmaj7, GbMaj7, GbΔ7, *Gb7)

243 1

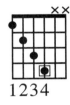

1234

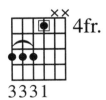

4fr.

3331

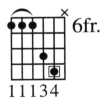

6fr.

11134

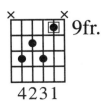

9fr.

4231

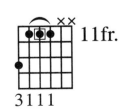

11fr.

3111

* Not recommended

33

G♭ minor 7
(G♭m7, G♭mi7, G♭min7, G♭-7)

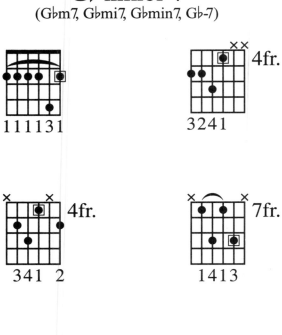

G♭ dominant 9
(G♭9)

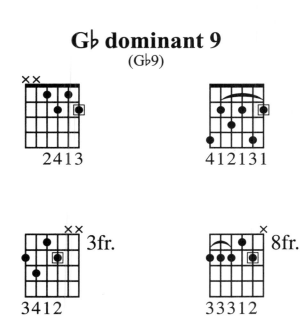

G♭ dominant 13
(G♭13)

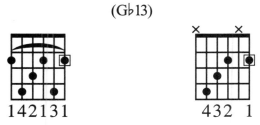

(G♭13)

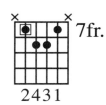

7fr.

2431

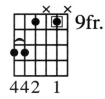

9fr.

442 1

G♭ major 6
(G♭6)

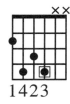

1423

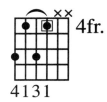

4fr.

4131

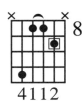

8fr.

4112

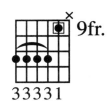

9fr.

33331

G♭ suspended 4
(G♭sus, G♭sus4)

114321

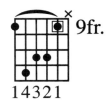

9fr.

14321

G♭ augmented
(G♭aug, G♭+)

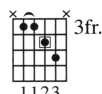

3fr.

1123

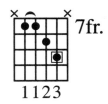

7fr.

1123

G♭ diminished 7
(G♭dim7, G♭°7)

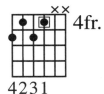

4fr.

4231

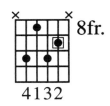

8fr.

4132

Key of G

G major
(G)

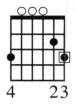

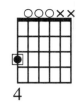

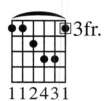

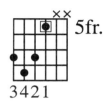

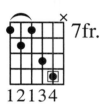

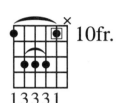

G minor
(Gm, Gmi, Gmin, G-)

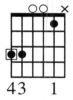

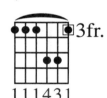

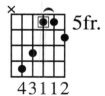

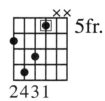

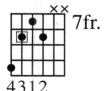

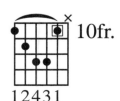

G dominant 7
(G7)

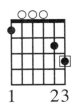

1   23

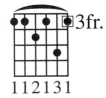

3fr.

112131

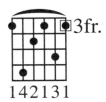

3fr.

142131

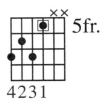

5fr.

4231

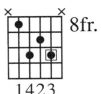

8fr.

1423

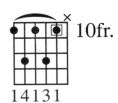

10fr.

14131

G major 7
(Gmaj7, GMaj7, GΔ7, *G7)

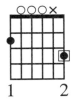

1   2

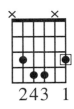

243 1

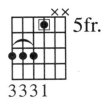

2fr.

1234

5fr.

3331

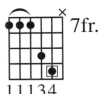

7fr.

11134

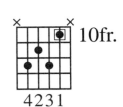

10fr.

4231

* Not recommended

G minor 7
(Gm7, Gmi7, Gmin7, G-7)

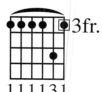
3fr.

111131

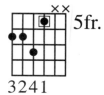
5fr.

3241

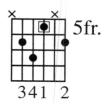
5fr.

341 2

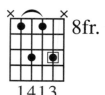
8fr.

1413

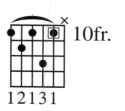
10fr.

12131

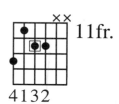
11fr.

4132

G dominant 9
(G9)

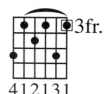

2413

3fr.

412131

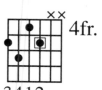
4fr.

3412

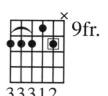
9fr.

33312

G dominant 13
(G13)

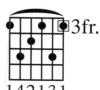
3fr.

142131

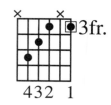
3fr.

432 1

(G13)

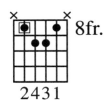 8fr.
2431

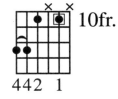 10fr.
442 1

G major 6
(G6)

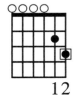
12

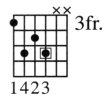 3fr.
1423

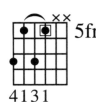 5fr.
4131

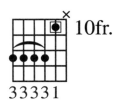 10fr.
33331

G suspended 4
(Gsus, Gsus4)

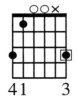
41   3

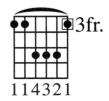 3fr.
114321

G augmented
(Gaug, G+)

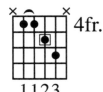 4fr.
1123

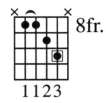 8fr.
1123

G diminished 7
(Gdim7, G°7)

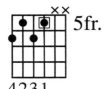 5fr.
4231

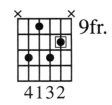 9fr.
4132

Key of A♭

A♭ major
(A♭)

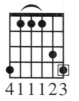

4 1 1 1 2 3

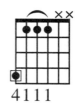

4 1 1 1

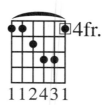
4fr.

1 1 2 4 3 1

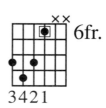
6fr.

3 4 2 1

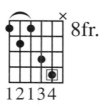
8fr.

1 2 1 3 4

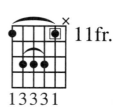
11fr.

1 3 3 3 1

A♭ minor
(A♭m, A♭mi, A♭min, A♭-)

4fr.

1 1 1 4 3 1

6fr.

4 3 1 1 2

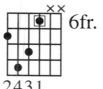
6fr.

2 4 3 1

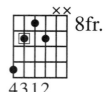
8fr.

4 3 1 2

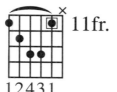
11fr.

1 2 4 3 1

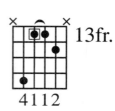
13fr.

4 1 1 2

A♭ dominant 7
(A♭7)

2111

4fr.

112131

4fr.

142131

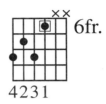

6fr.

4231

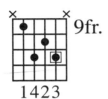

9fr.

1423

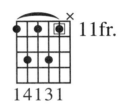

11fr.

14131

A♭ major 7
(A♭maj7, A♭Maj7, A♭Δ7, *A♭7)

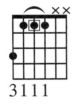

3111

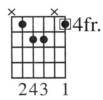

4fr.

243 1

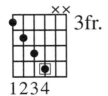

3fr.

1234

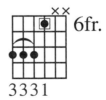

6fr.

3331

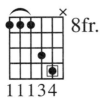

8fr.

11134

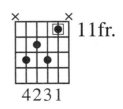

11fr.

4231

* Not recommended

Ab minor 7
(Abm7, Abmi7, Abmin7, Ab-7)

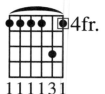

111131   4fr.

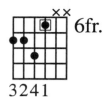

3241   6fr.

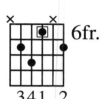

341 2   6fr.

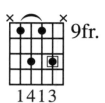

1413   9fr.

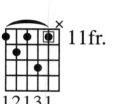

12131   11fr.

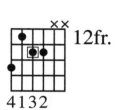

4132   12fr.

Ab dominant 9
(Ab9)

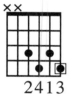

2413

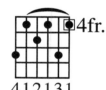

412131   4fr.

3412   5fr.

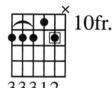

33312   10fr.

Ab dominant 13
(Ab13)

142131   4fr.

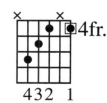

432 1   4fr.

(Ab13)

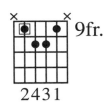

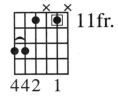

Ab major 6
(Ab6)

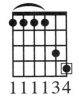

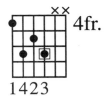

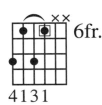

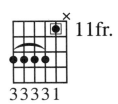

Ab suspended 4
(Absus, Absus4)

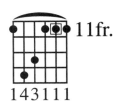

Ab augmented
(Abaug, Ab+)

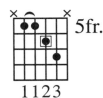

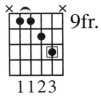

Ab diminished 7
(Abdim7, Ab°7)

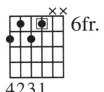

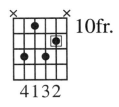

Key of A

A major
(A)

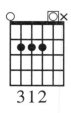

3 1 2

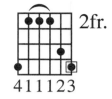

2fr.

4 1 1 1 2 3

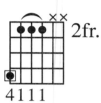

2fr.

4 1 1 1

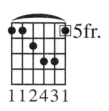

5fr.

1 1 2 4 3 1

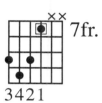

7fr.

3 4 2 1

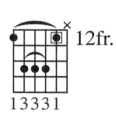

12fr.

1 3 3 3 1

A minor
(Am, Ami, Amin, A-)

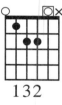

1 3 2

2fr.

4 1 1 2

5fr.

1 1 1 4 3 1

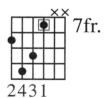

7fr.

2 4 3 1

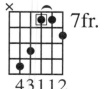

7fr.

4 3 1 1 2

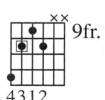

9fr.

4 3 1 2

A dominant 7
(A7)

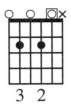

3 2

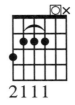

2111

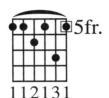

5fr.

112131

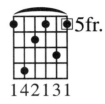

5fr.

142131

7fr.

4231

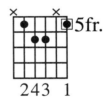

10fr.

1423

A major 7
(Amaj7, AMaj7, AΔ7, *A7)

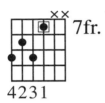

3111

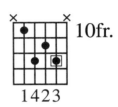

5fr.

243 1

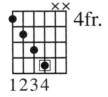

4fr.

1234

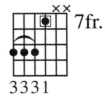

7fr.

3331

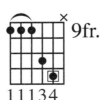

9fr.

11134

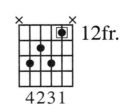

12fr.

4231

* Not recommended

A minor 7
(Am7, Ami7, Amin7, A-7)

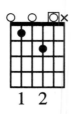

1 2

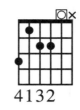

4132

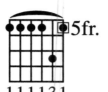

5fr.

111131

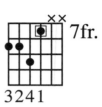

7fr.

3241

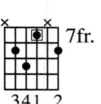

7fr.

341 2

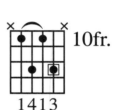

10fr.

1413

A dominant 9
(A9)

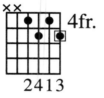

4fr.

2413

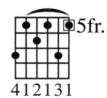

5fr.

412131

6fr.

3412

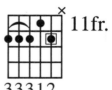

11fr.

33312

A dominant 13
(A13)

43 2

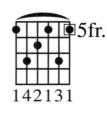

5fr.

142131

(A13)

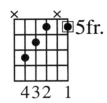 5fr.

432 1

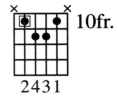 10fr.

2431

A major 6
(A6)

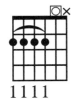

1111

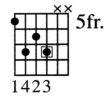 5fr.

1423

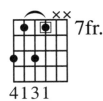 7fr.

4131

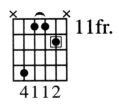 11fr.

4112

A suspended 4
(Asus, Asus4)

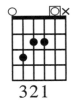

321

 5fr.

114321

A augmented
(Aaug, A+)

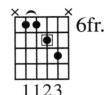 6fr.

1123

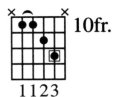 10fr.

1123

A diminished 7
(Adim7, A°7)

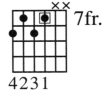 7fr.

4231

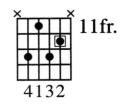 11fr.

4132

Key of B♭

B♭ major
(B♭)

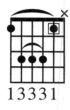

13331

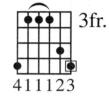

3fr.

411123

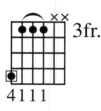

3fr.

4111

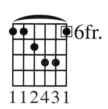

6fr.

112431

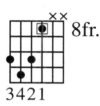

8fr.

3421

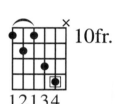

10fr.

12134

B♭ minor
(B♭m, B♭mi, B♭min, B♭-)

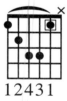

12431

3fr.

4112

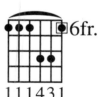

6fr.

111431

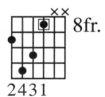

8fr.

2431

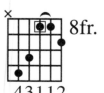

8fr.

43112

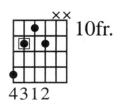

10fr.

4312

B♭ dominant 7
(B♭7)

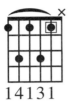

14131

2111

6fr.

112131

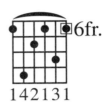

6fr.

142131

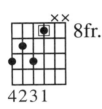

8fr.

4231

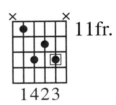

11fr.

1423

B♭ major 7
(B♭maj7, B♭Maj7, B♭△7, *B♭7)

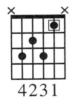

4231

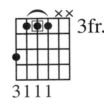

3fr.

3111

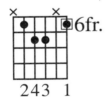

6fr.

243 1

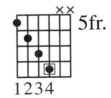

5fr.

1234

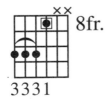

8fr.

3331

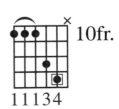

10fr.

11134

* Not recommended

49

B♭ minor 7
(B♭m7, B♭mi7, B♭min7, B♭-7)

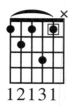

12131

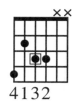

4132

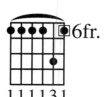

6fr.

111131

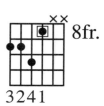

8fr.

3241

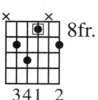

8fr.

341 2

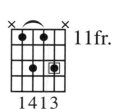

11fr.

1413

B♭ dominant 9
(B♭9)

5fr.

2413

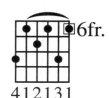

6fr.

412131

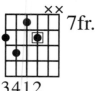

7fr.

3412

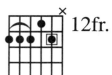

12fr.

33312

B♭ dominant 13
(B♭13)

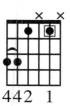

442 1

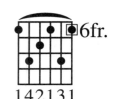

6fr.

142131

Bb13)

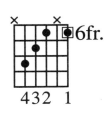

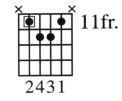

Bb major 6
(Bb6)

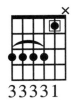

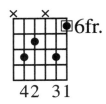

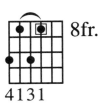

Bb suspended 4
(Bbsus, Bbsus4)

Bb augmented
(Bbaug, Bb+)

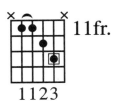

Bb diminished 7
(Bbdim7, Bb°7)

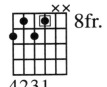

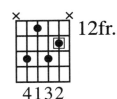

Key of B

B major
(B)

13331

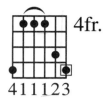

4fr.

411123

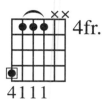

4fr.

4111

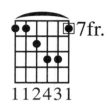

7fr.

112431

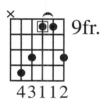

9fr.

43112

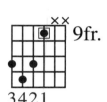

9fr.

3421

B minor
(Bm, Bmi, Bmin, B-)

12431

4fr.

4112

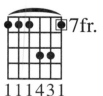

7fr.

111431

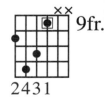

9fr.

2431

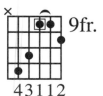

9fr.

43112

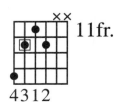

11fr.

4312

B dominant 7
(B7)

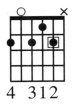

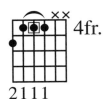

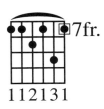

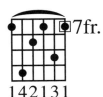

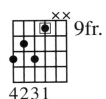

B major 7
(Bmaj7, BMaj7, BΔ7, *B7)

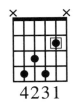

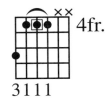

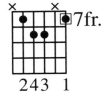

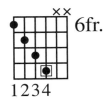

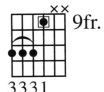

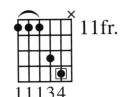

Not recommended

B minor 7
(Bm7, Bmi7, Bmin7, B-7)

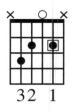

3 2   1

1 2 1 3 1

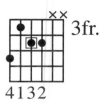

3fr.

4 1 3 2

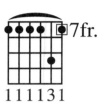

7fr.

1 1 1 1 3 1

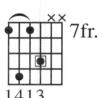

7fr.

1 4 1 3

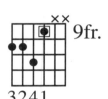

9fr.

3 2 4 1

B dominant 9
(B9)

3 3 3 1 2

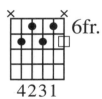

6fr.

4 2 3 1

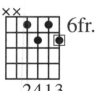

6fr.

2 4 1 3

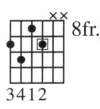

8fr.

3 4 1 2

B dominant 13
(B13)

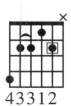

4 3 3 1 2

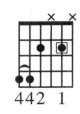

4 4 2   1

B13)

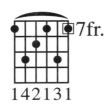 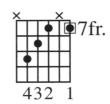

B major 6
(B6)

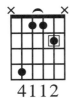 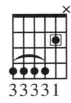

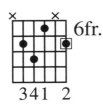 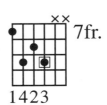

B suspended 4
(Bsus, Bsus4)

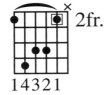 

B augmented
(Baug, B+)

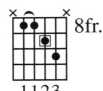 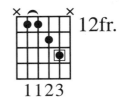

B diminished 7
(Bdim7, B°7)

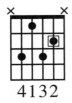 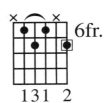

GUITAR TAB GLOSSARY
Tablature Explanation

Reading Tablature: Tablature illustrates the six strings of the guitar. Notes and chords are indicated by the placement of fret numbers on a given string(s).

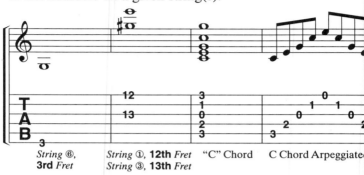

| *String* ⑥,
3rd *Fret* | *String* ①, **12th** *Fret*
String ③, **13th** *Fret* | "C" Chord | C Chord Arpeggiated |

Bending Notes

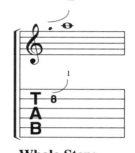

Half Step: Play the note and bend the string one half step.

Whole Step: Play the note and bend the string one whole step.

Prebend and Release: Bend the string one whole step, play it, then release to the original note.

Articulations

Hammer On: Play lower note, then "hammer on" to higher note with another finger. Only the first note is attacked.

Pull Off: Play higher note, then "pull off" to lower note with another finger. Only the first note is attacked.

Legato Slide: Play note and slide to the following note. Only first note attacked.

Rhythm Notation

Strum Indications: Strum with indicated rhythm. The chord voicings are found on the first page of the transcription underneath the song title.